Arise

Get Up and Get Moving

Rufus Adeoluwa Olodude

PUBLICATIONS

An Imprint of Sulis International Press
Los Angeles | Dallas | London

ARISE: GET UP AND GET MOVING
Copyright ©2024 by Rufus Adeoluwa Olodude. All rights reserved.

All rights reserved. No part of this book may be reproduced in any form or by any means without the prior written consent of the Publisher, excepting brief quotes used in reviews. For more information, contact the publisher at admin@sulisinternational.com.

ISBN (print): 978-1-958139-55-4
ISBN (eBook): 978-1-958139-56-1

Published by Keledei Publications
An Imprint of Sulis International
Los Angeles | Dallas | London

www.sulisinternational.com

Contents

Foreword i
Acknowledgements v
Introduction 1
Chapter 1 What Does It Mean To Arise? 5
Chapter 2 Obstacles of Rising 19
Chapter 3 Lessons From The Life Of Joseph 29
Chapter 4 Benefits Of Rising...............................35
Chapter 5 What You Must Have To Rise 45
Chapter 6 Why You Need To Rise 57
Chapter 7 What Is Holding You Forth? 65
Chapter 8 Come Out From The Shell..................71
Chapter 9 Get Back On Track 77
Chapter 10 Move On..83
Chapter 11 Stand Up and Save Others 89
Chapter 12 Confess, Proclaim And Declare It 95

This Book

is

Presented to:

....

By

....

On

....

This book is dedicated to my saviour, Jesus Christ.

Foreword

One of the hardest things to do as a man is getting up when things turn the other way around. We have been wired in our modern-day society to think that a failure is that man who fell because he failed but the truth is, a failure is not who failed but rather who failed to get up when he fell.

Nothing makes success possible like failing. A successful man without experience can be a threat. We don't become until we have either experienced one form of pain or the other. Scars can be proof that a man is on the right path. No matter how many times you have failed or fallen, refusing to rise is not a good option.

Rufus Adeoluwa Olodude, in his timeless book *Arise*, has shown deep secrets that make for a successful standing up again. Nothing is impossible to that man who can stand again. This twelve-chapter book is loaded with great insights that will pull you out of regrets and link you to the path where men whose past has disqualified them are made to stand out. Arise, it is still possible to become it.

I want to recommend this timeless book to everyone in every walk of life. It is time to Arise. Isaiah 60:1 reads

Arise, shine; for thy light is come, and the glory of the LORD is risen upon thee.

You are the display of the glory of the Lord. Hence, you must arise. God Bless you as you read.

—Prophet Ola Olayiwola
General Overseer, WordHouse International Ministry
Tanke, Ilorin, Kwara State
pastorolaministry@gmail.com

*

Arise is the product of the spiritual research and exploration of a lawyer, a scholar, and a research analyst, Barrister Rufus Adeoluwa Olodude. He has delved into the nature of man and his complacency (inability to arise and move forward) and also into the essence of God's call to man and his need to arise. Barrister Adeoluwa has been burning for God since he was in secondary school. He has been an organizer of Christian seminars, an editor of Christian magazines, and a teacher of the word of God.

I have gone through this book and discovered it is a lifelong Christian literature that will minister to the soul of every reader, especially the youth who would want to answer some questions in the context of this book. Questions such as: What does it mean to arise? Why do we need to arise? How do we arise? When do we need to arise? Who should arise? All these pertinent questions have been spiritually answered in this book with reference to biblical principles and philosophies. The scriptural quotations therein are compatible with the write-up.

I wish to let the readers know that God is a stimulus for him to write this book. This is because his prayer life and his study life have been remarkable. You have not made a mistake by laying your hand on the book to read because his ultimate goal is to preach the gospel and tell people to live a holy life. His desire for the gospel and for the downtrodden to be lifted is what gave birth to the book Arise. I am amazingly impressed by the content of this book.

For people who are thirsty for elevation and greatness in life, both spiritual and otherwise, *Arise* is the book you can read without distracting embellishments. Make it a companion in your journey in life. Read, read, and re-read for you to feel the impact and impart others, it is impactation for impartation.

Let me finally recommend this book to the general public, theologians, academicians, men of God, and youths who covet knowledge in all spheres.

—Pastor Ayo Olamoyegun
Christ Apostolic Church
Redeemer's Chapel District Headquarters
Egbejila Road, Airport, Ilorin, Kwara State
olamoyegunayo@gmail.com

Acknowledgements

First and foremost, I am profoundly grateful to God, the sustainer of my life, whose divine inspiration made the writing of this book, *Arise*, possible.

I would like to thank my parents and my lovely siblings for their unwavering support throughout this journey and their commitment to see it come to fruition.

I wish to express my deep appreciation to my cherished friend, Eniolaoluwa Awofolaju, who believed in the vision. Your unwavering support and faith have been invaluable. I am also grateful to Barr. Bukola Odu, Barr. Tobi Abisoye, and Deacon Wole Olatunde for their encouragement and belief in this project.

A special thank you goes to Busayomi Adekoya, who generously helped with proofreading and editing. Your meticulous attention to detail greatly enhanced the quality of this book.

Special thanks also goes to Sulis International Press, for providing the enabling environment to publish this book seamlessly

I must also acknowledge my spiritual father, Prophet Dr. E.O Alonge, whose teachings instilled in me the fear of God from childhood and guided my spiritual journey.

Additionally, I extend my heartfelt thanks to my pastors, Prophet Ola Olayiwola and Pastor Ayo Olamoyegun, for their spiritual guidance and support. Thank you all. Your contributions have been indispensable, and I sincerely appreciate every one of you.

Introduction

In every human journey, there comes a moment when we must confront the crossroads of stagnation and movement, of remaining in the shadows or stepping into the light. This pivotal moment is encapsulated in the powerful concept of Arise, which transcends mere physical movement to encompass a profound transformation of mind, spirit, and purpose. Arise is not just an action - it is a clarion call to change, growth, and fulfillment.

As the author of Arise, I invite you to see this book as more than a collection of words; it is a manifesto for personal and spiritual awakening. It is an invitation to break free from the chains of past hurts, disappointments, and limiting beliefs that hold us back. Drawing on deep wells of faith, scriptural insights, and practical wisdom, I encourage you, dear reader, to embark on a journey of self-discovery and empowerment.

To truly understand the essence of the term *arise*, we must look beyond the surface. Arising is about taking a leap of faith, standing up against the odds, moving forward despite challenges, and changing our thought processes to align with a higher purpose. It is about heeding wise counsel, voicing out when necessary, and knowing when to remain silent and listen. It involves a relentless pursuit of betterment through prayer and reflection. I open this book with a powerful exposition on what it means to arise, using Isaiah 60:1 as a foundational text: "Arise, shine, for your light has come." This scripture is not just a call to action but a promise of illumination and transformation. To arise is to embrace a new position illuminated by divine light, a position that cannot be hidden.

In the journey of rising, obstacles are inevitable. Throughout this book, I dedicated significant portions to identifying and overcoming these hurdles. From personal anecdotes to biblical stories, I illustrated how obstacles such as past hurts, bad company, and environmental limitations can impede our progress. However, I also provided the tools and mindset needed to navigate these challenges effectively.

The rewards of heeding the call to arise are manifold. Rising above our circumstances enables us to see beyond the immediate challenges and envision a future filled with possibilities. It fosters a stand-up mentality, allowing us to confront and overcome life's adversities with courage and resilience. More importantly, it cultivates a forgiving spirit, helping us to let go of past grievances and embrace a future of reconciliation and peace.

This book is not merely a passive read, but a call to action. I invite you to take tangible steps towards your transformation, emphasizing the importance of being available and useful, diligent in our pursuits, and dedicated to living a life of impact. The stories of biblical characters such as Joseph and David are timeless examples of how rising above our circumstances can lead to profound personal and communal benefits.

In essence, 'Arise' is a powerful guide for anyone seeking to break free from the confines of their current situation and step into a life of purpose and fulfillment. My insights and teachings provided a roadmap to not only understand what it means to rise, but also to live it out in every aspect of life. As you delve into this book, may you find the inspiration and strength to get up, get moving, and embrace the transformative power of arising in Jesus' name.

—Rufus Adeoluwa Olodude, LL.B, B.L, LL.M(OAU), P.GDE, ACIArb(UK)
adeoluwaolodude@gmail.com

Chapter 1
What Does It Mean To Arise?

The word 'arise' can be viewed from different perspectives. It is important to establish that to arise is an action word that means to change position. Isaiah 60:1 supports this interpretation: "Arise, shine, for your light has come". This scripture presupposes a change in position that occurs by an uplifting brought about by an illuminative light that is so conspicuous that it cannot be hidden.

To arise can also be seen as a process of moving from one status quo to a higher realm. It is important to note that this process is usually coupled with a determination to change position to achieve a set goal. You cannot rise if you do not have the requisite standing. Rising is a systematic determination of an increase that occurs over time until the zenith point is reached.

Can you imagine enduring emotional and physical trauma for an offense you did not commit? Or taking responsibility for the actions or inactions of another? Or giving your soul to a person who messed it up? How would you feel? I hear you say you would feel very upset about it. And the next time you see the person responsible for your predicament, I am sure you would not embrace him/her wholeheartedly.

No doubt, an average person with a normal intuition level will be uncomfortable seeing that person whose actions might have hurt him in the past, and if he is not careful, it will affect his relationship with other reasonable people in the future. It is even likely to trigger regression. Are you in that category? Are you emotionally and psychologically broken?

There can only be two sides to a coin; you can either be alive or psychologically broken. And if you are broken, you would no doubt be surrounded by psychologically broken people. Your life attracts those who can't offer you anything but can only sympathize with you. And really, you can't blame them because they have no solution to your predicament; they are also psychologically broken and piercingly hurt. Rather than offer you what will uplift you, they demoralize you the more with their counsel that adds no value.

It is apposite to examine Mark 5: 38

> *38 And he cometh to the house of the ruler of the synagogue, and seeth the tumult, and them that wept and wailed greatly.*

The above scripture relates to the death of the daughter of the Synagogue Ruler. Jesus had earlier been invited to pray for her, but unfortunately, before Jesus got to the house of the synagogue ruler, the daughter of the Synagogue ruler had died. When Jesus came to the Synagogue ruler's house, he saw a large crowd wailing.

It is a different thing to console, and it is another to wail. It is important to point out that we have got more wailers in this generation than consolers. Note that Jesus saw them weeping, and the King James Version went further to say that they wailed greatly. Most times, you discover that instead of people to help you out of your depressed situations today, they make you more depressed with their uncensored advice. Let's examine the next verse of the scripture.

39 And when he was come in, he saith unto them, Why make ye this ado, and weep? The damsel is not dead, but sleepeth.

How you would know the wailers and consolers/problem-solvers is by their utterances. Jesus said "Why make ye thus ado, and weep? The damsel is not dead, but sleepeth."

As can be seen above, you don't need people that will make you give up on yourself, you need people that will make you hope for better things. Jesus said emphatically, he is not dead, but he sleepeth. You don't need to listen to psychologically disgruntled people but listen to God's dictate.

Mind you, your present predicament gives some people joy that you have given up on your dreams, and they are ready to scorn you so that you can continue in your depressed state for life. Mark: 5:40

To arise, you need mentally purified associations whose mentality is right and sane in line with the word of God. To arise, you also need people whose faith is still living and not dead to stir you up. See Mark 5: 41-42:

> *41 And he took the damsel by the hand, and said unto her, Talitha cumi; which is being interpreted, Damsel, I say unto thee, arise.*
>
> *42 And straightway the damsel arose, and walked; for she was of the age of twelve years. And they were astonished with a great astonishment.*

Praise God!

We must know that to rise is not always a comfortable situation for the victim; it is usually coupled with strong determination against all odds that are attacking us to pull us down. Jesus rose the young lad with the company of the right people in the room. In essence, this means our association determines a whole lot about our rising and falling. Having the right association propels us to a place of rising that heals our souls.

We shall be considering the meaning of Arise in the following sub-heads:

To Take a Leap (Of Faith)

To arise can be seen as taking a leap of faith. What is a leap? Leap literally means to jump or soar as you may like to put it. For this discussion, I will say to leap means taking a risk.

Martin Luther King Jnr once said, that faith is taking a step, even if you don't see the whole staircase. If you must rise you must leap. We might be tempted to call it gamble but it's not gambling, it is exercising faith unusually. How would you see Abraham's decision to leave his tribe and kindred? It is taking a leap of faith. When you leap, you don't know what lies ahead, but you are sure of victory through God. You are, in essence, taking a risk, but in this context, you are exercising faith. Have you ever taken note when reading your Bible that when the pregnancy of John the Baptist met with that of Jesus, we were told that the pregnancy of John the Baptist leaped? This makes me understand that it is only those who are connected that can exercise this uncommon faith. Your connectivity to the source makes a sure way that helps you leap to a breakthrough.

Esther's experience in the book of Esther, Chapter 2 is a very good reference point in this circumstance. She was nominated to contest for the position of the Queen whereas she was a Jewish national. She is not fit to be selected as the Queen but she takes that leap of faith with the help of her uncle, Mordecai. Don't be carried away by the norm, take a leap. The norm can go in your favor. It was taboo to visit the King without his invitation, yet Esther leaped and although she was at a point afraid, she obtained the King's favor (Esther 5). Take a leap of faith, it is allowed once you are connected to the source.

One day, the Holy Spirit ministered to me to call someone. I was reluctant because the person I was to call could be difficult at times, and if you don't meet him in a good mood, you might be emotionally abused. I was compelled, so I took the leap of faith. Lo and behold, I got what I wanted from him. Take a leap of faith on that issue that is bothering you. You might have a good response instead of what you thought.

Have you tarried long in that position with no remarkable achievement that you can write about? Take a leap of faith. Is something not walking right in your life at the moment? Pray and take a leap of faith.

To Stand Up

To arise in this context is to see from another perspective. Have you ever considered that a person standing on a raised platform sees from another perspective things a person on the ground floor or level ground sees? A person on the ground floor might be myopic and possibly may not see far. It would be okay to say they might see faintly. The same applies to a person sitting down. Sitting may not allow him to see correctly, but a person standing up will have a projected and full view of things. Your thoughts may be totally out of place, but if you don't stand up, you may not be properly guided.

Standing up makes you different from the crowd. You may think where you are is God's final destination for your life, but if you don't stand up, you may not see the opportunities ahead of you. Sitting down in your comfort zone may not help you realize your full potential; stand up from that comfort zone and see a new light.

You may be sitting in darkness, but if you don't stand, you may not realize that you need to make necessary amends towards the light. It was only Joshua and Caleb who stood up in their thinking about possessing the promised land. I once had this myopic mindset when I was growing up until I stood up and started to see things differently that I began to get new results. Some people have the mindset that they are slaves and not free-born; if you have taken note, they usually live all their lives miserable and end up regretting. Imagine if Joseph had carried the mentality that his master had power over everything and could do as he wished to him. He would have accepted the proposal of Potiphar's wife. He might even voluntarily surrender himself to his master's wife, that maybe sleeping with her will make his life better. But Joseph had a stand-up mentality that wouldn't allow him to take an ignorant disposition that would destroy his future. If we must arise, we must have this stand-up mentality that will keep us on our feet.

I remember back in my undergraduate days when people were forming fake allegiances with lecturers to graduate and make good grades. I had this mentality that if God could help me to this point, I trust Him for the rest. Information had it that those who made higher grades were so many that they had to reduce the number. I didn't know anybody but because I had a stand-up mentality trusting in God, I came out with the best grade. For you to arise and shine, you need a stand-up mentality.

To Move On

To arise could also mean to move on and progress further, no matter what one has been through. This is usually characterized by a state where all seems hopeless and helpless. It is a point in one's life that all seems bleak by the surrounding circumstances. It is a time when disappointment upon disappointment overshadows one's path, and one's journey seems gloomy. Job was in this kind of situation. His future became bleak, but until he moved on by praying for his friends, he didn't record any breakthrough. Moving on despite surrounding circumstances is a hard thing to do, especially in a disgruntled period, but moving on is the only solution to conquer. Have you been cheated on? It is time to move on. The bible recorded that after David cried and cried concerning his sick child given birth to by Uriah's wife when he was told that the child was no more, he stopped crying, worshipped God, and ate (2 Samuel 12: 19-21). In essence, he moved on. After grieving because of disappointments, the next point of call is to move on.

I could remember a particular point in my life when I was disgruntled and disappointed about all around me. I so much trusted in man that I placed my life at their whims and caprices. I felt cheated, and I was very hurt when I realized that their lips were full of deceits, but after coming across a book by Joel Osteen that encouraged me to move, I decided to move on. If we grieve all day, it won't heal our wounds but only worsen them. Feelings of hurt are usually like a shock that pierces deep into one soul. This explains the reason some find it difficult to relate with people after being hurt.

I have discovered that moving on is the only healing peel that can heal our souls in such periods. I recently offered a programmeme outside my field, and it was recorded that I failed a particular course that I so cherished in this programme. To tell you the extent of how I felt, I had to abandon the programme for close to a year because I was unable to comprehend the fact that I failed and I was to re-write that paper. After grieving and hurting for a while, I registered for the course again, and I aced it. That you failed is not a dead end. You need to move on.

To Change Position/To Change a Thought Process

Have you noticed that a car parked in a spot for a long while with its tyres on may wear out over time? Some lives are like that. They have stayed in one position for too long, and their mentality has become archaic and barbaric, which has retarded their rising. We usually say in law, that a custom is repugnant if it fails to be in line with natural justice, good conscience, and equity. It is desirable at times that, before we can arise, we need to overhaul our mentality by changing position.

Zacchaeus changed position. He climbed the sycamore tree to see Jesus, knowing fully well that his short height wouldn't have allowed him to see Jesus. Have you been getting the same result repeatedly? It may be because you have not changed your position. It may even be that you have limited God to a particular angle, and he is saying that this is not my way, that He wants you to change position. Staying in a position outside the will of God may not take us to God's designed destination for our lives. Is your life so static that you find it difficult to arise to be what God wants you to be? You may have to change your position or your thought process to arise.

To Heed Advice/Instruction

If Adam knew the importance of the instruction given to them not to take the forbidden fruit, he would have refused and kept his peace and tranquility in the Garden of Eden. Also, if the small prophet knew the magnitude of keeping the instruction given to him by God, he would not have heeded the advice of the old prophet. So many destinies have been destroyed because they failed to heed advice from God. Good counsel allows us to rise, while bad ones send us to the early grave.

Most times, out of sheer ignorance, we discard good counsel and embrace folly. Moses made the mistake of striking the rock with his rod rather than touching it. We rise steadily when we constantly keep to godly counsel. Have you been disobeying a counsel that seems unpalatable but will help your life? It is better you heed to it to rise. I am sure Samson was warned by his parents repeatedly, but he refused to heed their counsel, and that led to his early ruin. If you want to rise, you must learn to heed Godly counsel.

To Voice Out

To rise is to voice out. A problem shared is a problem half-solved. A lot of people die in silence today just because they cannot voice out. I don't usually encourage the dissolution of marriage, but recently, someone very close to me called to confide in me about what she's going through in her marriage. I could perceive this as a life and death issue, and if care is not taken, we could lose her by the acts of domestic violence being unleashed on her by her spouse. I was able to talk her through it, and she dared to tell her immediate family members that took the necessary steps. As you are aware, there are so many victims of domestic violence who died out of ignorance. Had it been she didn't voice out, she might have died a sorrowful death. For us to arise, we need to voice out. Is your relationship going out of hand, and you are keeping quiet for the fun of it? It is time you talk to an elderly person or an expert in that field to advise you.

I could also remember a friend who once confided in me about her boss trying to harass her at her place of work. Her voicing out made me give some necessary advice that saved her. You should not be enmeshed in silence. You should speak out. Voicing out propels your rising. If we fail to voice out, we might be a subject of ridicule and depression all through our lives. People who fail to voice out are usually victims of psychological trauma that takes time before healing. If you want to rise and don't want to be an object of ridicule, you must voice out.

To Keep Quiet And Listen

At times, to arise means to keep quiet and listen. The Bible in Psalm 85:8 says "I will listen to what God will say, for he will speak peace to his people, let them not return to folly". In our quietness lies our deliverance at times. We may find it difficult to hear from God if we fail to keep quiet and listen. If we listen to what God will have us do, we will get ahead. Maybe you have prayed but not seeing results yet, pause and listen. One of the things that helped David was his ability to listen to what God would have him do each time. We do ourselves a lot of good when we listen to rise. A lot of people have run out of oil because they failed to listen. My reading partner back in my postgraduate days, so much loved a yoruba song that usually comes to mind, *enu ose, enu ose, ariwo ko ni music, empty barrel lo ma n p'ariwo* meaning it is empty barrels that make the loudest noise. In essence, there are times we need to be quiet to listen to the next step.

To Yearn In Prayers

To arise also means to yearn in prayers. The Bible says when I shout, my enemies will turn back. Murmuring does not bring deliverance, only fervent prayer does. The Bible says the effective prayer of the righteous avails much. When our prayers are right before God, deliverance comes in with speed. We yearn in prayers when we are no longer comfortable with our present state. It is at that point we thirst for a raise.

The sure way to make deliverance happen is to cry unto God. It must be noted that Jabesh cried to God for deliverance and the Lord heard him. We must understand that our prayers are channels to our rising and actualizing what God wants us to be. It is because we don't know the usefulness of the open cheque that we possess, that is why we tarry long unnecessarily in seeking human favors. Do we know that attracting the favor of God automatically sends down the help of man? The Bible says we should ask anything in his name and he promised to oblige us. That happens to be the best offer given to us ever. Have you prayed today?

Chapter 2
Obstacles of Rising

In this chapter, we shall be examining the obstacles to rising. So many people desire to rise but their progress has been hindered by some external forces. This chapter seeks to open our understanding to such things that may be hindering our rising.

Sharing Your Dream With The Wrong People

You will agree with me that the mistake Joseph made that opened his life up for battles was sharing his dream with the wrong set of people. Saved for the mercies of God, that actually could have cost him his life. Who do you share your dreams with? Are they the right set of people or the wrong set?

Many have ignorantly shared their dreams with the wrong set of people which has stagnated their journey in life. You would have discovered that after sharing your dreams and aspirations with some particular set of people, they whittle them down while some make sure they do not manifest. I once shared my dream of going for a master's programme with a professional boss who at that time, had bagged one master's and had another in view in the field of law. He discouraged me, that I didn't need a master's degree. As far as he is concerned, it is not necessary. This is a person who travels far and wide presenting papers and seminars, and at that time, he was almost completing his second master's degree in the field of law. I was disappointed, to say the least.

Who do you share your dreams with? I usually warn my protégés against sharing their dreams with a tormentor in the form of a mentor.

One of the strategies the enemy of Joseph used to gain access to his life was through his inability to keep his dreams and vision to himself. When you share your dreams with the wrong set of people, you get the wrong results, while sharing your dreams with the right people gets you positive results. I remember that I once shared a vision with someone about a business idea, and he discouraged me and gave me another line of business. Behold, the business idea he gave me didn't last. When God gives you a dream, he expects you to carry it out with the specifications he gave you after you have done your feasibility study. He doesn't need another man's approval. The story of the young and old prophet quickly comes to mind. The Lord gave the young prophet an instruction to go deliver a message for the king and further instructed him not to eat on his journey. The mistake the young prophet made was sharing God's message with the old prophet. After making the mistake, he should have asked God for directional wisdom to deal with the old prophet but he didn't do that either. The mistake of young people of today is that we are always in a haste to share our dreams and visions with the wrong set of people, whereas they seek to lead us astray from the plan and purpose of God. I have learned countless lessons on this point that space won't permit me to share. We must learn not to be in a hurry to share our dreams with the wrong people. It is one of the obstacles to rising, and we need the Holy Spirit to direct us. The Bible says in Psalm 32:8 TLB:

I will instruct you(says the Lord) and guide you along the best pathway for your life: I will advise you and watch your progress.

Thus, we need the Holy Spirit as our sure guide against sharing our dreams with the wrong set of people. This is the only antidote to overcome this obstacle.

Obstacle Of The Flesh

The flesh has been part and parcel of us since time immemorial. Apostle Paul, at a point, said, "Who shall deliver me from this flesh?" That, at times, he wants to do good but bad manifests. The closest definition to the discourse at hand sees flesh as the fallen and corrupted human body with all its lusts.

Another definition states that flesh is that which is contrary to the spirit. Flesh in this context could simply be defined as immorality.

One of the things that helped Joseph was his being able to conquer flesh at the tender age of seventeen. It is a pity young people are exposed to immorality at a tender age. I once counseled a young girl who is still in secondary school and under the age of 17, already exposed to immorality. The funny thing was that it was difficult to convince her since she saw immorality as a norm. Interestingly, we read in the bible that Joseph was able to conquer flesh at age Seventeen which shows his level of discipline at that young age.

How many of us can conquer flesh today? The male folks now see sex as a ritual they must perform before marriage, and the female folks are not left out. The most painful thing is that unknowingly, evil covenants are being initiated and destinies contaminated, which usually inhibits the rise of most youths out there. Joseph was a focused youth. Had he agreed to sleep with his master's wife, he would have ended his career as Chief Servant in the house of Potiphar. Have you noticed that anyone who demands to have carnal knowledge of someone unlawfully is not always sincere, and it is not in their habit to fulfill their concocted promises or make their victims more prosperous than themselves? The best they offer is to turn their victim into a readymade slave. It is not in their habit to help that person achieve the full potential of what God made that person to be. Joseph fled.

Although he was unjustly imprisoned, he attained his full potential in God. Is this obstacle of the flesh hindering you from rising? Have you slept with countless men/women whose destinies may have unknowingly caged your destiny? You can still come to Jesus today and rededicate your life to him. Are you the type that sleeps with everything in skirts? Your story can be rewritten as you get washed in His precious blood.

The obstacle of the flesh usually raises its venom at a future date when it is time to start reaping. A colleague once told me about an uncle who wanted to rape her some time ago but she was able to overcome him. She said recently, she saw him in a car park, and from his looks, his life appeared very unpleasant to behold. She struggled with refreshing her memory about who the man was. It is a pity he wasted his life pleasing the flesh. Because he could not control his flesh, it ruined him. We must subject our flesh to the voice of God if we want to rise.

Obstacles of Past Hurts

Another piercingly dangerous obstacle affecting this generation is the obstacle of past hurt. This obstacle has hindered so many from rising to their full potential. This obstacle can lead to depression if care is not taken. It presupposes that because someone has hurt me in the past, I will not move ahead and it's better to accept defeat as the final say than to move on. When someone's mind is hinged on past hurt, it takes the grace of God to minister to that person to change his/her ways. If we fail to arise in this state, we can't be made whole.

Past hurt is a cankerworm that has eaten deep into the contemporary day and builds a network of discord in the victim that makes every other person a faulty individual. It discourages trust but encourages fear in the victim. It is an obstacle because the victim sees everyone as the same person as the person that hurt him/her in the past, thereby making it difficult to be helped by God. It bridges the gap between God-sent helper and the victim and this hinders one's rising. Having come across people who suffer from this obstacle, if you are not patient, you may find it difficult to relate with them and be of help to them. It is usually very difficult to accommodate such people in your space.

There is a saying that 'hurting people hurt people'. If you have encountered someone who is enmeshed in past hurt, you will observe that the spirit in them appears like a demon that drives away every passerby. When the seed of past hurt is not quickly uprooted, it hinders one's rising and if care is not taken, it will be late before one realizes his/her mistakes. So many people enmeshed in past hurt later regret their actions and if wisdom is not applied, they hurriedly fall into wrong hands due to unnecessary pressure at the wrong time. As a result of their poor past experience, they usually find it very difficult to relate even if they are in dire need of help. This neglect may cost them a fortune. No doubt a person who can't relate may die in silence if care is not taken. It is very important that the cord of past hurt is broken and we live our lives purposefully as our master wants it, if we want to arise.

Obstacle of Bad Company

Another destructive obstacle is bad company. The Bible says bad company corrupts good manners. If you keep the wrong company as friends, it will be extremely difficult to rise. The story of Prince Ammon and Tamar is very instructive here.

> *Prince Absalom, David's Son, had a beautiful sister named Tamar. And Prince Amnon (her half brother) fell desperately in love with her. Amnon became so tormented by his love for her that he became ill. He had no way of talking to her, for the girls and young men were kept strictly apart. But Amnon had a very crafty friend- his cousin Jonadab (the son of David's brother Shime-ah).*
>
> *One day Jonadab said to Amnon, "What's the trouble? Why should the son of a King look so haggard morning after morning?"*
>
> *Well, Jonadab said, "I'll tell you what to do. Go back to bed and pretend you are sick; when your father comes to see you, ask him to let Tamar come and prepare some food for you. Tell him you 'll feel better if she feeds you." 2 Sam 13: 1-5 TLB*

It is important to point out that the Bible referred to Jonadab as a very crafty friend, which presupposes that he is a bad influence. In his expertise as a crafty person, he was able to provide a destructive solution to Amnon's lustful desire to have carnal knowledge of his half-sister. Who is your friend? What type of company do you keep? If one is not very careful, the company one keeps can ruin him/her. Amnon's friend in his craftiness, provided an abominable way to satisfy his friend's lustful desire which later led to Amnon's ruin. Who knows whether Amnon was destined to be great but due to bad advice by a bad friend, he lost his throne?

The company we keep has a lot to do with our future. This is one reason we should be careful while making friends. I have come across friends who discourage one from a good vision but end up championing the same vision for another. We must know this for sure, some people are not true friends but are looking out for miserable companions that they can always have around. Until we realize this, it will be difficult to rise purposefully into our full and optimum potential in God. Amnon yielded to the advice of Jonadab and pretended to be ill just to have her half-sister. Have you also lied due to a bad friend's advice just to have what does not belong to you? I always say that for every premeditated evil intention, there is always approval by bad company. Who is your friend? They may be a bad influence on your rising.

Environmental Obstacles

The environment we find ourselves and operate in is very crucial to our rising. If the environment we find ourselves in is not designed for us, we can't prosper. Some of us live in an environment that is too uncomfortable and too remote for us to rise. I believe God sees that if Abraham lived all his life in Ur, he might not be as prosperous as He has designed for him. He had to instruct him to leave his people and kindred. If your environment is too remote for your rising, you cannot be announced. Abraham was announced immediately after leaving Ur. If we are not located in the right place, we cannot be helped.

A lot of destinies are wasting away today because they are not rightly located. It is a pity we sometimes derive pleasure in forcing ourselves into places where God has not called us to function. I usually say not everyone is called to the ministry but it is a pity we find people who want to squeeze themselves into it when God has not called them. It may interest you to know that some might even function well as church members. When we operate in an environment God has not called us, we should be ready for doom. Ignorance has led some people to operate in an atmosphere God has not destined for them. Thus, we must have a personal relationship with God, to know exactly what God wants from us per time so that we are not pushed around following another man's frolic. When we operate in his will and his purpose (desired environment), we are deemed to rise in glorification and not destruction. Are you operating in the atmosphere God wants you or following another man's frolic?

Obstacles of Character

Character defines who a person is. Our character is our identity. Our character attracts and at the same time, dispels. I have come across people whose character ordinarily cannot hold a relationship with another person. When a person's character is faulty, everything about him/her will be faulty. Vashti would have retained her position as Queen but due to her character deficiency, she lost her crown. Gehazi would have taken over from Elijah but due to his character deficiency, he lost his throne. Judas Iscariot could have done much more than other disciples after Christ's resurrection but due to his trait of rebellion, he lost his office.

One of the most common traits of character deficiency in our generation is pride. Any person with the trait of pride doesn't usually go far. When our character is not in line with God's precept, we miss the path to our rising. For us to rise, we must imbibe good character by being true children of God and not mere churchgoers. Thus, we must covet the fruits of the spirit so that our lives will attract favor if we want to arise and make an impact.

Chapter 3
Lessons From The Life Of Joseph

In this chapter, we shall be considering the difficulties of rising, particularly using the lessons that could be learned from the story of Joseph. As we have considered quite some perspectives on the concept of rising, this chapter shall tilt further to expantiate on the lessons from the life of Joseph. It takes a conscious mind to arise and tap into the numerous blessings attached thereto. Hence, someone with a foreclosed mindset would not see the need to arise, due to the difficulties on the way. It takes a strong and systematic determination from a conscious mind to jump up from the pit of psychological trauma and rejection to move into a renewed mindset according to God's purpose.

The story of the young Joseph is a typical example that can be carefully examined as it relates to this discourse. It is often rare to see a young person with a renewed mindset like Joseph who is aware of God's purpose for his life at that tender age. Joseph was shown the master plan of God for his life and he was aware he would someday rise. Though he didn't know how his rising would come, he was sure of a glorious future.

Out of sheer ignorance, he shared his dream with his brothers who happened to be his immediate enemies.

Let's examine Genesis 37 verses 5-7:

> *5 Joseph had a dream, and when he told it to his brothers, they hated him all the more. 6 He said to them, "Listen to this dream I had: 7 We were binding sheaves of grain out in the field when suddenly my sheaf rose and stood upright, while your sheaves gathered around mine and bowed down to it.*

It is important to reiterate from the above scripture that Joseph had been hated by his brothers even before sharing the dream he had with them, but the mere fact that he shared his dream made them hate him more. Do you know some people don't know about God's plan for your life but they are already jealous of your giant strides? And the mere fact that they now know about you, they are looking out for ways to pull you down, so that you won't get to God's desired destination. That's why you always need God's help.

A careful examination of verse 7 reveals God's purpose was for Joseph to rise above his peers. It stated thus "We were binding sheaves of grain out in the field when suddenly ***my sheaf rose and stood upright***".

It is instructive to know what a sheaf means to have a proper understanding. A sheaf is a bundle of grain stalks bound up in a bundle. So in essence, what Joseph saw in his dream was that his harvest of grains was massive in height and it rose beyond that of his brothers. Whereas his brothers' harvests were very minute in substance, and according to Joseph's dream, they were altogether bowing down for his bountiful harvest. In essence, his sheaf stood out and rose above all others while the others were paying homage to his sheaf. It is only a person who becomes successful (arises from shame, setback, past hurt, and rejection) that they pay homage to. It is not in the habit of people to pay homage to a failure. That is why, no matter how young a boss is in an organization because his sheaf rose and stood upright in that position of authority, he/she will enjoy due respect from his subordinates.

His brothers, having a good understanding of the meaning of the dream, were afraid of his rising and would prefer to get rid of him than bow down for their junior brother.

Let's further examine the verses below:

***23** So when Joseph came to his brothers, they stripped him of his robe—the ornate robe he was wearing— **24** and they took him and threw him into the cistern. The cistern was empty; there was no water in it.*

***25** As they sat down to eat their meal, they looked up and saw a caravan of Ishmaelites coming from Gilead. Their camels were loaded with spices, balm and myrrh, and they were on their way to take them down to Egypt.*

***26** Judah said to his brothers, "What will we*

*gain if we kill our brother and cover up his blood? **27** Come, let's sell him to the Ishmaelites and not lay our hands on him; after all, he is our brother, our own flesh and blood." His brothers agreed.*

***28** So when the Midianite merchants came by, his brothers pulled Joseph up out of the cistern and sold him for twenty shekels[b] of silver to the Ishmaelites, who took him to Egypt.*

We could deduce from the above that Joseph's siblings thought it wise in themselves that it is better to frustrate God's plan than allow him to rise. They wanted to kill him by throwing him into a pit, but they later thought about it and decided to sell him for twenty shekels of silver to Ishmaelite traders. They forgot that God's purpose can only be delayed but cannot be denied. They had forgotten that all things work together for good to those who love God and are called according to His purpose. When you are denied, you don't need to be troubled or perplexed. You must know some disappointments are divinely orchestrated by God to bring out your best. Information once had it that a child of God was denied an admission that should ordinarily be given without stress. He was disappointed because he had all the requisite qualifications needed. Although disappointed, he didn't let that discourage him but pressed further. He took up the courage to apply for another which was better off than the first. He was fortunate to be selected, and he came out tops. What a mighty God we serve! Next time you are rejected, do not be discouraged, but press further.

You are aware that Joseph encountered so many challenges before he could confidently rise to the palace as the Governor of Egypt. He rose from the pit of death to slavery and thereafter, to a servant in the house of Potiphar. Because of his steadfast love for Yahweh and fear of God, he rejected the offer by Portiphar's wife to sleep with her, and because of his righteousness, he was punished unjustly, dumped and forgotten in prison for an offense he didn't commit but God did not forget him.

Joseph wasn't depressed nor did he curse God because of his life hurdles, rather he made himself a solution wherever he found himself. Are you depressed about your present state? What have you been doing to occupy your mind and develop yourself? Are you waiting for a miracle you are not properly groomed for? You need to be groomed. The ignorant Joseph later became the wise Joseph who was highly sought-after after his slave-to-prison experience. You are meant to acquire new values and jettison the old mentality for you to permanently rise and be relevant. Note, that it was after the University of Life that Joseph attended, that his mentality changed. How did I know this? His slave-to-prison experience was a requisite qualification that helped him to properly manage the affairs of Egypt. If we want to rise, we must first rise for Christ in righteousness and humility.

Joseph recognizing his enemies, did not fret. He knew them but they couldn't recognize him. Despite his special treatment towards them, they still couldn't recognize him. He dined with his brothers who thought he wouldn't rise. The dream he had came to pass, they bowed for him, and they became his subject. He exercised his position of authority on them as he had foretold. He wasn't too quick to tell them who he was, he was now matured and learned. By the time he revealed his identity, they had already given him the due respect he deserved.

Let's examine Genesis 45 verse 3:

> *And Joseph said unto his brethren, **I am Joseph**; doth my father live? And his brethren could not answer him; for they were troubled at his presence.*

When all was said and done, Joseph announced his appearance before his brothers. What I could infer Joseph said in essence was this…

> *I am Joseph, whom you sold for twenty shekels of silver. Well, despite all your efforts to frustrate and hinder God's plan, **I rose** and I'm thankful! I thank you for helping me to discover purpose in a foreign land.*

You need to accept to rise from everything holding you down from fulfilling your destiny. Could it be your mentality, your circle of friends, works of flesh, laziness, lackadaisical attitude, or comfort zone syndrome? You need to rise and never return. Joseph rose, even after all that his brothers did to him; Joseph rose from his past. He rose to forgiveness rather than hatred.

Chapter 4
Benefits Of Rising

Following the last chapter, a lot of lessons could be learned that would be of help to the present generation. Joseph didn't hold a grudge, pass unnecessary aggression, or abuse God and resort to fate despite his challenges; he did everything with gladness and open heart. He exerted his best at every opportunity; even in prison, he became a solution. Your predicament is not a password to hurt people around you. It is a phase to express thanksgiving, for the morning of restoration is at hand. Howbeit, if we maintain an atmosphere of thanksgiving arising from that atmosphere of confusion and embrace God, it comes along with our breakthrough. Premised on the above, we shall be considering the benefits of rising from the exemplary life of Joseph. They are as follows:

It Makes Us See Beyond The Now

If Joseph had dwelt on the past hurts, mistakes, setbacks, and failures of how he was sold unjustly and accused wrongfully at Potiphar's house, he wouldn't have been able to get to God's desired destination for his life. Without minding the circumstances that placed him in the dungeon of life, Joseph was busy utilizing his giftings in the prison as if nothing happened to him. He didn't relent because of the trials and temptations. He was able to say boldly to the cupbearer that he should remember him when he gets out of prison. He knows one day, he will be vindicated and set free. At this point, he was seeing beyond the setbacks and ugly circumstances life served him. He didn't surrender to a sit-down mentality because he knew one day he would get out of prison, so he was networking with the people destiny brought his way. We need to see beyond the now, have futuristic goals, and refuse to retire in our comfort zone because of the flimsy excuses that we suffered from past hurts and rejection.

Have you been hurt? Move on. Hurt is not a basis to shut out and shut down everyone in your life and tag them as bad. If Joseph had tagged everyone as a bad person and entered his shell, he would not have been able to use his giftings or see himself as a solution to someone's problem and encounter his destiny helper. Regardless of what people do to you, remember you are a solution to other people's problems. You have been equipped to serve as a leap to stir other people's faith. Joseph was able to see beyond the now; even Jesus on the Cross was able to see beyond the now. He said, Father, forgive them for they know not what they are doing (Luke 23: 34). If we can arise from that shock and pitiable situation, we will be able to see better opportunities and drive towards what would fit us into His purpose. Remember, until Joseph rose and harnessed his giftings, he wasn't strategically made ready to be remembered. Rising makes us see opportunities in obstacles.

It Makes You Have a Stand-Up Mentality

Another benefit of rising is that it makes us have a stand-up mentality. For instance, Potiphar's wife wanted to lure Joseph to sleep with her, but Joseph said, 'How can I do this and sin against God?' He wasn't concerned about the pleasure and the enjoyment that comes with sleeping with the wife of his boss rather, he had a stand-up mentality that doing this would make him sin against God. Rising from past hurts should make you stronger rather than bury you in delusion and the dead end of accepting every dick and harry opportunity that comes your way.

I encountered a lady who allowed someone to take advantage of her in exchange for comfort and pleasure because of rejection by her family members. This experience opened her up to an indecent lifestyle. Albeit, because she was suffering from an inferiority complex, she accepted fate and became an object of pleasure to men who came her way but who were not ready to have her hand in marriage. In moments of rejection, it is better to run to God, open up to Him, find a safe place of refuge, and also approach people who have integrity and the right value system for support. These will help you have a sure footing with a stand-up mentality that will help your worth, rather than accepting a life of ridicule. The Bible made us understand that our worth is more than rubies (Proverb 3:15).

I have seen a situation where someone approached a selfish prophet, who in turn collected all her money and also married her. In moments of rejection, to arise and to have a stand-up mentality, you have to locate a trusted household of faith and be careful of how you let people play with your emotions. In these moments, your imbalanced emotion can become a tool in the hands of destiny manipulators if you are not careful. Be wise!

It Makes Forgiveness Flow In Your Heart

Another benefit of rising to God's marvelous light is that it encourages healing and forgiveness. When Joseph saw his siblings, forgiveness freely flowed from his heart. This was made possible because he has risen from that pitiable situation to a more renewed mentality. A similar situation happened when Jacob saw Esau, who cheated on his brother and stole his birthright. Jacob was at first jittery at Esau, but Esau told him he didn't need his cattle, and that God had also blessed him.

But Esau said, "I already have plenty, my brother. Keep what you have for yourself." (Gen 33:9)

This renewed mentality will help forgiveness to flow naturally. If we could rise from that past hurt and embrace the spirit of love in Christ Jesus, forgiveness would be an easy ride. This would so much help our healing process and make us that which God has called us to be. Failure to rise to forgiveness, may lead to retardation, stagnation and retrogression. When Joseph finally met his brothers, he chose forgiveness, recognizing the hand of God that has made his life beautiful. This act of forgiveness not only brought peace to Joseph, but ultimately saved his family from famine. The rejected stone could later be the cornerstone, if we embrace a forgiving heart and move on (Psalm 118:22).

It Makes You Remove Any Price Tag On Yourself

Some people have placed price tags on everything that comes their way and see every opportunity as an avenue to exploit and drain. If someone has hurt you in the past, it is not an opportunity to pass aggression on to others such as suitors, or exploit business partners and clients. This was not the case with Joseph in the prison. He voluntarily helped destinies inside prison by interpreting dreams for them without collecting a dime. He didn't place a price tag on himself. He used the gift of God freely without expecting anything in return (Matt 10:8).

We have shepherds who should tend the flock but who demand exorbitant offerings before they can pray for their flock. If only we could learn from Joseph and how he patiently stayed on course, we would know God is the rewarder of those who diligently seek him. If Joseph had placed a price tag on himself, do we think the cupbearer would remember him? Even if he does, he would say to the king that I know of someone but he charges exorbitantly. Hence, the king won't take him seriously. His reward would have been limited to only money. If you have risen from that past hurt and rejection, you won't spill anger on those who know nothing about your predicament. You treat everyone with kindness without expecting anything in return and God will reward you and surprise you beyond your imagination. This was the story of Joseph; he interpreted the king's dream without expecting anything in return and God made it possible that the King made him the prime minister in a foreign land. God's ways are not our ways. We mustn't place price tags on ourselves.

As a lady looking up to God for settlement, you mustn't place a price on yourself because all that glitters is not always gold. So many ladies have missed out on God's plan by excessive demands on their supposed spouse or looking down on people who come their way. I know of someone that if her man should tell her that he didn't have enough resources to meet her demand, she would start misbehaving, thereby, making life miserable for him.

In my interview with a renowned man of God, Rev. Oset, he said money answereth questions money asked, and that godly virtues cannot be purchased with money. If you want to rise and shine in God, you will understand that it is a wrong mentality to place price tags on yourself.

Character Development Through Trials

The hardships Joseph endured refined his character. We could see as a fact that Joseph came out as gold. He learned valuable lessons on leadership, interpretation of dreams, and crisis management. These experiences prepared him to lead Egypt as the Prime Minister during a time of great famine, showcasing how adversity can build strength and wisdom.

It Makes It Easy For Your Giftings To Announce You

If we can rise to the marvelous light of our God and forsake those things that can hinder our rising, it makes it easy for us to express our giftings. If Joseph was depressed and dejected by his experiences - how they sold him to Ishaemalites traders and how he got to the prison unjustly when his master's wife wanted to lay with him and he fled, he would have buried his giftings and exalted his scars more than his gifts. However, he made use of his giftings gladly and that made way for him. If we rise from depression, rejection, and past hurts, we will be able to use our giftings which will make room for us in unexpected quarters.

It Gives You a Voice Over Your Contemporaries Who Don't Wish You Well

We become role models to people in the world when we rise from self-pity and past hurts which will make room for us and give us a voice above our enemies. Joseph was able to tell his contenders to their faces *this is me, the Joseph you sold. I have fulfilled destiny; I am no more what you called me. I am God's masterpiece. I hold no grudges against you. You thought you could delay God's plan but I rose by the capacity Yahweh bestowed on me.*

It Makes You a Selfless Mentor

Misery companions would only make things worse by their counsel, but someone who is broken and has risen to his marvelous light with a renewed mindset would give you selfless counsel that would propel you into your rising. I have a mentor who always looks out for the best in people and makes them realize it. It is not as if he is mandated to do it, but he has taken it up as a responsibility to impact people. If you hurt people because you have been hurt, you are not wise. If you have been hurt, there is a reason for you to rise to marvelous light. Joyce Meyer, a renowned tele-evangelist and author was abused from a very tender age by her father. You won't hear Joyce Meyer preach hate or revenge. This is a typical example of a person that life has dealt with multiple times but she preaches peace to the brokenhearted. She derives joy in lifting other people and making them see the glorious future rather than burying people in their past hurts. If you can rise, even sinners would come to your marvelous light and you could groom them to the standard God wants for them.

It Makes You a Saviour Rather Than a Problem

The moment you rise, you become a solution to other people facing similar situations rather than a problem. One of the dangers of persons who fail to rise from past hurts and rejection is that such persons are prone to depression which makes them inflict pain and manipulate other people's thoughts to promote their selfish desires. This can lead to depression and violent activities.

By developing resilience, finding opportunities within limitations, and utilizing our gifts, we can rise above adversity and create a better future for ourselves and those around us. Joseph's journey from a betrayed son to a powerful leader serves as an inspiration for anyone facing difficulties, offering the promise that even in the darkest of times, rising above can lead to a brighter tomorrow.

It Helps In Forging Stronger Relationships

Joseph's reunion with his brothers and his forgiveness towards them is a testament to the power of reconciliation and strong family bonds. Despite their betrayal, Joseph chose to forgive and support them during the famine. Rising above grudges and past hurts helps to forge ahead stronger, and build more meaningful relationships that can lead to personal fulfillment and a supportive network. Strong relationships are crucial for emotional well-being and success. We should work towards resolving conflicts and building bridges with others. Forgiveness and understanding can transform relationships and provide a solid support system.

Chapter 5
What You Must Have To Rise

"Unless we are determined to arise, God will not arise"

In this Chapter, we shall be considering two major bible characters, David and Joseph. David and Joseph went through rejection, hurt by their relatives, and all manner of vices. To the extent that King Saul, whom David had been useful for at a point, was looking for David to Kill him. We could recall that David was employed to play harp for Saul in order to relieve him of his infirmities. Not to talk of Joseph, who was betrayed by his siblings when he was all out for their cause - to check on them as instructed by his father to see how they are faring in the bush-tendering flock (Gen 37;13). They had earlier plotted to kill him for no just cause, save for Reuben who jettisoned the idea with the intention of saving him and persuaded them to throw him into the pit, in order to get him rescued later. His brothers went ahead to strip him of his coat of many colors, and they threw him inside an empty well, not mindful of what could befall him inside, such as snakes and other harmful animals

(Gen 37:20). He was sold to the Ishmaelites traders for twenty shekels of silver due to jealousy by his brothers so that he won't rule over them (Gen 37;28).

Also, in the case of David, he was betrayed by his son, Absalom. At a point, his son tried killing him (2 Sam. 15-19). David was faced with battles roundabout, but despite all these and many more challenges, David and Joseph never forsook Yahweh. David was even referred to as a man after God's own heart.

Let's examine the qualities possessed by these two characters that we need to imbibe to arise and shine to enjoy God's best.

Availability And Usefulness

David happened to be very useful to his household and didn't entertain a life of liability. Despite being the youngest of the sons of Jesse, which ordinarily should make him pampered, he didn't allow himself to be pampered. It is also important to note that, being the youngest didn't foreclose his sense of reasoning to accept defeat and be lazy. He was very useful and was also a problem solver at every given point in time. God expects that we should be useful and be problem solvers, not minding any situation, position, or strata we find ourselves in. For instance, David made himself available to be sent on an errand to his siblings. At that point, he inquired what would be done to the person who conquers Goliath. He made himself available to be used not minding what could happen to him even when his older ones opposed him, he didn't relent (I Sam 17:26).

Joseph also was available, useful and dutiful at his post. The bible recorded in Genesis 39: 2-6 NLT:

The Lord was with Joseph, so he succeeded in everything he did as he served in the home of his Egyptian master. Potiphar noticed this and realized that the Lord was with Joseph, giving him success in everything he did. This pleased Potiphar, so he soon made Joseph his personal attendant. He put him in charge of his entire household and everything he owned. From the day Joseph was put in charge of his master's household and property, the Lord began to bless Potiphar's household for Joseph's sake. All his household affairs ran smoothly, and his crops and livestock flourished. So Potiphar gave Joseph complete administrative responsibility over everything he owned. With Joseph there, he didn't worry about a thing—except what kind of food to eat!

Joseph was first appointed Personal Attendant, later Master of Household and Property, then Administrative Head over everything owned by Potiphar. Even while in prison, he was available to solve other people's problems by interpreting their dreams (Gen 40; 1-19). The Bible further recorded in Gen 39:22-23:

But the LORD was with Joseph, and shewed him mercy, and gave him favour in the sight of

*the keeper of the prison. And the keeper of the
prison committed to Joseph's hand all the pris-
oners that were in the prison; and whatsoever
they did there, he was the doer of it.*

He maintained an open mind and didn't allow his past to affect his future. This made it possible for him to be appointed the prime minister. To rise to the fullness of Christ, we should be available, useful, and dutiful. God will not multiply a lazy man or a person who is thinking less of himself; God will only increase someone who is not held down by past hurt but maintains a free spirit and is open-minded, available, and useful.

Diligence

We mentioned that David and Joseph were useful because they allowed themselves to be used by God to serve as solutions. David allowed himself to be a shepherd to his father's flock. You will agree with me that taking care of his father's flock is a great task that requires due diligence and sacrifice. 1 Sam 17:34 recorded the testimony of David before Saul.

*And David said unto Saul, thy servant kept his
father's sheep, and there came a lion, and a
bear, and took a lamb out of the flock.*

The above exemplifies a lifestyle of diligence, dedication, and commitment. Even Joseph was diligent in taking care of Potiphar's household (Genesis 39: 2-6). Interpreting dreams for his colleagues in the prison shows diligence. It's only a person who is diligent in the service of the master that God can give revelation. If we want to rise, we must be determined to be committed to whatever we do.

Inquisitiveness And Sensitivity

The young David was very inquisitive to situations begging for answers around him. 1 Sam 17:26 stated as follows:

> *And David spake to the men that stood by him, saying, What shall be done to the man that killeth this Philistine, and taketh away the reproach from Israel? for who is this uncircumcised Philistine, that he should defy the armies of the living God?*

No wonder he asked the men on the battlefield for the reward to be given to the person who conquers Goliath. Though his brothers dissuaded him, he didn't keep quiet or mute till he got the answer he sought.

If we want to arise and take dominion, we must be spiritually sensitive and inquisitive to questions begging for answers around us. This will lead us aright in our quest to arise and take dominion. It is recommended that we ask questions before we enter into contractual relationships and even marital relationships on anything we are unclear about. The refusal of some people to ask questions has caused damaging effects.

A True Worshipper

It is important to note that, a true worshipper of God knows how to invite the presence of God into situations. This explains the reason why David was invited to play the harp to relieve Saul of his infirmities (1 Sam 16:23). We must learn to be a true worshipper in the service of God because as we worship God, we invite God into situations, and help us to conquer battles in the quest towards arising and taking dominion.

Brave Ambassador

God expects us to be His brave ambassadors whenever we are faced with dreaded situations. David saw the mighty Goliath and was still very brave to confront him. Surprisingly, he stated in 1 Sam 17: 45-47 thus:

Then said David to the Philistine, Thou comest to me with a sword, and with a spear, and with a shield: but I come to thee in the name of the LORD of hosts, the God of the armies of Israel, whom thou hast defied. This day will the LORD deliver thee into mine hand; and I will smite thee, and take thine head from thee; and I will give the carcases of the host of the Philistines this day unto the fowls of the air, and to the wild beasts of the earth; that all the earth may know that there is a God in Israel. And all this assembly shall know that the LORD saveth not with sword and spear: for the battle is the LORD'S, and he will give you into our hands.

We need to be brave, if we want to arise and function where God has called us to function. We need not entertain any fear but brace up like David did when he confronted Goliath.

Living Faith

It is important to infer further that David was a man of faith, to the extent that he affirms the existence of Yahweh as the living God in the face of the battle with the Philistines. He told Goliath to his face, that he came against him in the name of the Lord of Hosts, the God of armies of Israel whom he has defied. He affirmed his living faith by saying unequivocally in 1 Samuel 17: 46 that:

This day will the Lord deliver thee into mine hand, and i will smite thee, and take thine head from thee; and i will give the carcases of the host of the Philistines this day unto the fowls of the air, and to the wild beasts of the earth; that all the earth may know that there is a God in Israel.

This was a fantastic confession and the Lord God approved it. We must prepare to operate in the realm of living faith no matter the situation we are passing through if we want to arise and take dominion from that state of rejection and shame.

Dedication

The lifestyles of David and Joseph showed that dedication, faith, and hard work can lead to remarkable achievements. Today, countless individuals from modest backgrounds rise to prominence in various fields, emphasizing that your origin does not limit your potential. The former Minister of Finance, Mrs. Nkojo Iweala, is a very good example in this regard. Her dedication and passion opened unimaginable and remarkable doors for her at the World Bank. We must not relent and settle for defeat if we want to rise.

Living a Life of Impact

Recognizing and pursuing a greater purpose provides a sense of fulfillment and direction. Whether it's through your career, community service, or personal endeavors, striving to make a meaningful impact on others' lives, as David and Joseph did, leads to a more rewarding and purposeful life.

As king, David united the tribes of Israel and established Jerusalem as the nation's capital. His leadership had a lasting impact on Israel's history. Joseph's strategic planning during the years of plenty ensured Egypt's survival during the subsequent famine. His leadership not only saved countless lives but also strengthened Egypt's position in the region. Effective leadership and the ability to influence others are critical in today's world. Rising to leadership positions, whether in business, community, or politics, allows you to effect positive change and leave a lasting legacy just as David and Joseph did.

Forgiving Spirit

David showed mercy to Saul who sought to kill him, and later to Saul's family, demonstrating the power of forgiveness and reconciliation. In 1 Samuel 24:6, David stated thus;

> *And he said unto his men, The LORD forbid that I should do this thing unto my master, the LORD'S anointed, to stretch forth mine hand against him, seeing he is the anointed of the LORD.*

Joseph forgave his brothers who sold him into slavery (Gen 50: 15-21). This act of forgiveness restored his family and healed old wounds. Forgiveness and reconciliation are vital for personal and societal harmony. Rising above grudges and extending forgiveness can mend relationships and create a more positive environment. In today's context, leaders who promote reconciliation contribute to social cohesion and stability.

Ability To Learn And Improve Character

David faced numerous trials, including facing Goliath and fleeing from King Saul, who sought his life. These challenges formed his character, preparing him to be a wise and just king.

Joseph endured betrayal, false accusations, and imprisonment. These experiences honed his resilience, wisdom, and leadership qualities, making him an effective leader in Egypt.

Trials and tribulations build character. Just as David and Joseph emerged stronger from their struggles, facing challenges today can develop your resilience, patience, and problem-solving skills. These traits are invaluable in both personal and professional realms.

Ability To Recognize And Seize Opportunities

David seized the opportunity to fight Goliath when others were afraid. His victory catapulted him into the eye of the public and set the stage for his future kingship. Joseph interpreted Pharaoh's dreams when no one else could. This pivotal moment showcased his unique talents and led to his rise to power. Opportunities often arise amid challenges. Being prepared to seize these moments, like David and Joseph, can lead to significant breakthroughs in your career or personal life. Today, those who innovate and adapt during crises often find themselves ahead when the dust settles.

Resourcefulness

Joseph's ability to interpret dreams proved invaluable during the Egyptian famine. He used his foresight to prepare the nation, saving countless lives. This translates to the importance of vision and planning. By anticipating challenges and taking proactive steps, we can not only secure our success but also contribute to the well-being of those around us.

By applying the lessons gleaned from David and Joseph's stories, we can navigate difficult times, unlock our full potential, and achieve our goals. Rising above adversity is not just about overcoming a single challenge, but about becoming a better version of ourselves in the process.

The stories of David and Joseph from the Bible provide timeless lessons on the importance of rising above adversity. Both figures faced significant challenges yet emerged victorious through resilience, faith, and perseverance. These narratives offer profound insights applicable to contemporary life, demonstrating why it is essential to rise and overcome life's obstacles, thus making a positive impact on our lives and the lives of those around us.

Chapter 6
Why You Need To Rise

This chapter examines the reasons we must rise from the syndrome of rejection, psychological trauma, past hurts, and depression that are holding us back and have hindered us from being the person God called us to be. It serves as a liberation manual to consider when giving thought to whether to remain in depression and accept defeat, or embrace God's marvelous light that relieves us of our worries and helps us stand upright as Joseph did.

We shall be examining the reasons one after the other. Isaiah 61:1 is very instructive and shall be our focal scripture in this chapter. Hence, it is necessary to reproduce the same.

Isaiah 61:1 says

> *The Spirit of the Lord GOD is upon Me, because the LORD has anointed Me to preach good tidings to the poor; He has sent Me to heal the brokenhearted, To proclaim liberty to the captives, and the opening of the prison to those who are bound.*

We Have Been Commissioned To Preach His Word

God has commissioned every one of us to be gospel proclaimers. A person who is hurt cannot be in the right frame of mind to preach the gospel of Christ. A person who feels dejected and rejected will find it difficult to pass across the message of hope to others. There is a saying that a person who is hurt also hurts people. This is true. A person whose mind has not been renewed according to God's purpose will be critical about things. This is the reason why we need to rise and refuse to let issues of life drive us away from fulfilling the task the master gave us.

If a person's behavior and character are not stable, it will probably not attract people to Christ. If care is not taken, due to depression he/she failed to manage, the person would be a bad example to the body of Christ. Hence, his/her character will dispel people away from the way of salvation. I have seen Christians who are hurt and could not help but pass aggression to others, and the fact that due to their state of mind, they exhibit bitterness. If such psychological trauma is not quickly addressed, it could make them develop psychological imbalance, which would make them hostile in character and dealings. They could even be terror to any organization they find themselves.

Consequently, if we are yet to allow Christ to work through us, we can't pass across a message of hope. The hope message is sweet when we have got an understanding of His words beyond the letters and we are led by His Spirit to flourish in all things. If we want to experience the benefits of salvation, we would have to arise and allow ourselves to be used by God. The Bible said our revealing is awaited. If that is so, for us to manifest in His glory and make a world of difference, we need to shed down every weight the devil has placed on our heart that presents us as a bad light to the gospel of Christ; or every weight of depression and past hurts that has foreclosed our eyes of understanding to see the marvelous light in His Kingdom and be a proclaimer.

If the world is watching us, then we are to come out boldly for Christ and embrace him. He would give us rest. You need to arise because God needs you.

To Cease Living A Miserable Life

You would agree with me that a hurt person is an angry person. Hurting people don't usually portray happiness. We ought to understand that God has promised us a life of peace and tranquility. Howbeit, the bible confirms that there will be tribulations in the world but we should be of good cheer, He has overcome the world (John 16:33). This explains why we have to arise to live a peaceful and accommodating life, and above all, be at peace with all men (Romans 12:18). If we are determined to arise and embrace his yoke, which is easy and his burden which is light, we will be happy (Matt 11:30).

Howbeit, hurting people are comfortable living a life of seclusion. A life of seclusion if not well managed, can lead to depression and suicidal attempts. God has said none shall lack his mate (Isaiah 34:16). This is not limited to a life partner, but also includes who to communicate and share your burden with. You need to rise from that life of seclusion to see the beautiful side of life. You are not the first person to make mistakes or be rejected. You need to rise and walk up to someone who has integrity and is spirit-filled, who can lead you back to the old rugged cross. Someone who can help you attain your standing in God to make you strive to be the perfect person God wants you to be.

To Be Able To See The Future And Not Be Critical

Over time, I have had courses to interact with some hurting people. They are usually very critical of issues and little things throw them off balance. They also, view things irrationally. However, if you are one of such, it is important to examine yourself to see where you are missing it. Constructively appraise your acts and omissions in time past. In addition, you need to see the future from a new lens and be in it, rather than accept fate. Be in the future and stay patient enough to let God lead you and not emotions.

To Cease Making Terrible Decisions

If we don't allow God in our lives, but rather allow grudges, bitterness, and anger to encompass it, we cannot experience the fullness of God. We can't expect to tap into His knowledge and divine wisdom when we entertain rage and past hurts, it will lead us to make hasty decisions that are against His will and purpose for our lives. When our mind is renewed, we think like God. The Bible says those who are led by the Spirit of God are called the sons of God (Romans 8:14). Hence if our mind is renewed according to His will, we are properly guided to make the right decisions. Howbeit, we make hasty and nasty decisions whenever we are hurt. God wants us to experience Him per time. In this light, we need to shed the weight of hurt feelings that have beclouded our eyes of resounding decisions. David refused to Kill Saul while he was angry. I have seen people who have lost wonderful relationships because they couldn't control their anger and I have also seen people who have lost valuable connections due to the words of their mouth.

To Win Souls For Christ

I said earlier on, that it is difficult to win souls for Christ if we are not yet broken. A message given by someone who is not broken, might not have enough potency to carry out the efficacy of Christ's power. These days people are first attracted to us through our Godly lifestyle both in thought and actions. If we are to win souls for Christ, our minds must be clean, clear, and genuine. A person who doesn't have a good personal relationship with his colleagues would not be able to effectively deliver the message of hope. If you want to win souls for Christ, your mind must be right with God and the works of the flesh should not be made evident.

To Heal The Brokenhearted

Experience they say, is the best teacher. You would be able to encourage others if you were once a victim of abuse, rejection, past hurts, and other vices and you have been able to heal. Joyce Meyer is a very good example in this regard. She is doing great exploits healing the brokenhearted with her words of power and wisdom through her messages and books. You need to arise because you are commissioned to lift others and walk them through the healing process with God's word and how God has helped you to conquer. I am always very happy to share my academic pursuits with people, and I love to walk them through succeeding in theirs. I am a living testimony to academic success, so I don't shy away from sharing my testimony. I also encourage people in other areas of life. Your triumphant experiences are a testament to God's goodness and they could heal the brokenhearted and give them hope for the future. If you see someone who doesn't have a stable relationship, you can use your experience to walk them through to conquer that stage of their life. If you don't arise, you can't have a testimony to encourage others or win souls for the master.

To Open The Prison To Those Who Are Bound

Recently, I shared my past experiences with someone to liberate him from the guise of evil. The person has been caged for a while, he doesn't know what to do. I discovered he needed an orientation to change his mentality and perspective. Our mentality can bind our rising. If we arise from unpalatable situations without resorting to fate, we become better evangelists to free the captive. Your past experience and how you conquered are testaments that you have once been in such a situation that is somewhat life threatening but God set you free by His mercies. I believe Paul and Silas, if they were privileged, could share their experiences in the prison and how they conquered. You could also be a victim that has been bound by the enemy, not necessarily a physical prison, testimony of people who have triumphed can be of help to conquer your challenges. You have been commissioned to open the prison to those who are bound, hence you need to arise.

To Proclaim Liberty To The Captives

Similar to the above, your past experiences could help you proclaim liberty to the captives. For the Bible says the captives shall be delivered. You need to arise in the power of His might so that you can use the power that made you conquer to proclaim liberty for God's children in similar situations. You need to arise in order to deliver those under the captivity and siege of the enemy who are suffering a similar fate you once experienced. Elisha escaped the shame he would have encountered from the people who thought the absence of his master would expose him to a life of reproach. He proved them wrong, and he got a double portion of Elijah's power that silenced his contenders. He parted the Red Sea and did many other landmark miracles. Hence, it is important you arise to proclaim liberty to the captives.

Chapter 7
What Is Holding You Forth?

In the Gospel of John chapter 5, there is a story of a man who had been an invalid for thirty-eight years, lying by the pool of Bethesda. This pool was believed to have healing powers, and many sick and disabled people waited for the stirring of its water by an Angel, hoping to be the first to enter and be healed. When Jesus saw the man and learned of his long-term condition, he asked him, "Do you want to get well?" This simple yet profound question and the man's response offer valuable insights into what might be holding us back in our own lives.

When Jesus asked the man, "Do you want to get well?" (John 5:6), it may have seemed obvious. Why wouldn't he want to be healed? Yet, the question forced the man to confront his true desires and motivations. Often, we need to ask ourselves if we genuinely desire change or if we've grown comfortable in our discomfort. The fear of the unknown can be so paralyzing, making it easier to stay in the familiar though unsatisfactory circumstances.

Reflecting on what we truly want is the first step towards overcoming what holds us back. I have identified some of the things that hold us back below.

Past Hurts/Psychological Trauma

So many times our past experiences and psychological trauma hold us back from being that which God has called us into. The Man at the pool who had no one to help him whenever the water was stirred, was explaining his ordeal to Jesus even while he had the opportunity to be made whole instantly. "While I am trying to get in, someone else goes down ahead of me" (John 5:7). The scripture referenced above demonstrates that his past experiences limited his mentality when he met Jesus. He had believed that his present predicament was the normal trend of things and he had accepted his fate. At a point in my life, I had accepted an awkward fate and this affected my rising. If we don't arise, past hurts, rejection and psychological trauma can hold us back. Hence, the need for us to arise and come under the authority of His marvelous light.

Embargo

Embargoes are external obstructions in our way to success and they limit and hold us back from fulfilling our destiny. It could sometimes take the form of laws, decrees, proclamations, and regulations. In John 5:7b, the man by the pool stated categorically that 'while I am coming, another steppeth down before me.' This is an example of an embargo in human form that had restricted the man by the pool from being whole. An embargo is a distraction that holds us back from rising.

Every embargo that has placed our life in jeopardy is hereby removed for our sake in Jesus' name.

Incapacity

At times, what is holding us back might come in the form of incapacity. Incapacity is a mental or physical inability to perform or do something we should ordinarily be graced for. The impotent man answered Jesus, "Sir, I have no man, when the water is troubled, to put me into the pool."

Incapacity may be to different degrees, it could be due to a lack of connection or financial constraint. Hence, we need to arise to break free from every power that has incapacitated us. Until Jesus helped the incapacity of the man at the pool, he was unable to break free.

Excuses/Procrastination

Excuses are baseless reasons and assertions that restrict us from accepting responsibility and make it difficult for us to take proactive steps towards our rising. The man's explanation for why he hadn't been healed is an example of making excuses. He focused on the barriers rather than seeking other ways to achieve his goal. Excuses can become significant obstacles in our lives. They often mask our fears and insecurities. Acknowledging and overcoming these excuses requires honesty and a willingness to confront our limitations. Hence, we become whole when we jettison excuses that hold us back from fulfilling destiny and arise to the fullness of Christ.

Loneliness

Another thing holding us back is loneliness. One tool employed by loneliness is depression. Depression makes it difficult to rise to the fullness of Christ as the mind is clouded. The impotent man answered, "Sir, I have no man. " This shows the man has been fighting his battles alone without support from anyone. In situations like this, it could be somehow frustrating to rise. If loneliness is not properly handled, it can lead to suicide. Loneliness is one of the mechanisms used by the devil that could hold us back from achieving God's desired destination for our lives.

Mentality

Believing in the possibility of change is essential, no matter how hard it is. Faith in ourselves, in the process, or a higher power can provide the strength needed to overcome obstacles. We must cultivate a mindset that change is possible and we can achieve anything. Once healed, the man at the pool had to leave behind his old life and embrace a new reality. It required a significant shift in his identity and daily routine. Change often requires us to let go of old habits and embrace new beginnings. It can be daunting, but it is necessary for growth. We must embrace the opportunities that come with change and view them as steps toward a better future.

Refusal To Act

Jesus' command to "Get up! Pick up your mat and walk" emphasized personal responsibility. The man had to take action to experience his complete healing. Failure to act is one of the issues that has made it impossible to rise to his fullness in Christ Jesus. Taking personal responsibility for our lives is empowering. It shifts the focus from what we can't control to what we can. Identify areas where you can take control and make proactive choices that lead to positive change.

The story of the man by the Pool of Bethesda challenges us to examine whatever is holding us forth. Are we clear about our desires? Are we making excuses or taking initiative? Do we have the faith to believe in change and the courage to embrace new beginnings? By addressing these questions and taking personal responsibility for our actions, we can overcome the barriers that hold us back and move toward a more fulfilling life.

Chapter 8
Come Out From The Shell

The story of Moses no doubt, is one of the most inspiring narratives in the Bible that symbolizes tenacity, persistence, doggedness, freedom, authority, and divine predestination. Moses' evolution from the shy shepherd boy who resisted his fate as the liberator of the Israelites out of the bonds of Egyptian oppressors is one of the most profound lessons of coming out of one's shell of fear, self-doubt, and circumscribed potentials. This chapter explores these lessons and encourages us to step out of our comfort zones and realize our potential.

Moses was born Hebrew but raised as an Egyptian prince. This dual identity caused internal conflict, but he eventually embraced his Hebrew heritage when he killed an Egyptian who was beating a Hebrew slave (Exodus 2:11-12). This act marked the beginning of his journey towards his true purpose.

What is your Identity?

Many of us struggle with issues surrounding identities, feeling torn between different expectations and roles. It is crucial to know that embracing our identity and who we truly are, is the first step in coming out of our shells. Accepting and owning our identity, which God called us, even if it differs from societal expectations, is crucial for personal growth and fulfilment. When God called Moses to lead the Israelites out of Egypt, he was full of doubt and fear; He questioned his abilities and worried about how others would perceive him (Exodus 3:11, 4:10). God reassured him by promising His presence and providing signs to prove His power. We should always know that God is always there to help us at every point in time when we feel insufficient. 2 Cor. 12: 9 declares:

And he said unto me, My grace is sufficient for thee: for my strength is made perfect in weakness.

Jeremiah also exhibited fear about his identity. He was reluctant to forge ahead to do what God would have him do, and God had to remind Jeremiah of who he was. It is instructive to examine the scriptures to appreciate this point further. Jeremiah 1;5-7 stated thus:

Then the word of the LORD came unto me, saying, Before I formed thee in the belly I knew thee; and before thou camest forth out of the womb I sanctified thee, and I ordained thee a prophet unto the nations. Then said I, Ah, Lord GOD! behold, I cannot speak: for I am a child. But the LORD said unto me, Say not, I am a child: for thou shalt go to all that I shall send thee, and whatsoever I command thee thou shalt speak.

Howbeit, fear of rejection, past hurts, and doubts often hold us back from pursuing our dreams and taking bold steps. Recognizing these feelings and seeking reassurance, whether through faith in God, self-affirmation in the word of God, or support from others, can help us overcome them. Stepping out despite our fears is essential for growth and success.

Despite his initial reluctance, Moses accepted God's call to leadership. He confronted Pharaoh and led the Israelites through the Red Sea and towards the Promised Land. His leadership transformed not only his life but also the lives of millions. We should know that God does not call the qualified, He qualifies the called. Jeremiah also exhibited fear, but through him, God performed signs and wonders. That you once failed or have no experience is not a prerequisite for not succeeding. Abraham was asked to leave his kindred to where God would show him, he didn't hesitate. Although Abraham did not have an idea of the terrain, he succeeded. If God has revealed to you the 'where', don't hesitate to take the bold step to move. Don't let past rejection, setbacks, and trauma close you up in your shell, instead, come out of your shell. Take up that job, write that book, start that programme, enter into that relationship, and start that project because your identity is in God. You have no reason to fear.

You Must Be Ready To Face Challenges

Howbeit, leadership opportunities and taking up obligations toward leaving your comfort zone often come with significant responsibilities and challenges. Accepting these opportunities is essential, even when we feel unprepared, can lead to profound personal and global transformation. Stepping into that role, not being mindful of challenges that may hinder us, can help us to make positive impacts and fulfill our potential. Moses faced numerous challenges, from the plagues of Egypt to the complaints and rebellions of the Israelites. Each challenge taught him valuable lessons in patience, faith, and perseverance (Exodus 14-17).

In addition, challenges and setbacks are inevitable in life. Rather than retreating into our shells, we should view these difficulties as opportunities for learning and growth. If you have suffered rejection at a time, that does not mean there is no light at the end of the tunnel. Every obstacle can teach us something valuable and help us become more resilient and capable.

Moses' journey was driven by a higher purpose – to fulfill God's promise to Abraham and lead the Israelites to freedom. This divine mission gave him the strength to persevere through countless trials (Exodus 3:16-17).

You Must Have a Purpose And a Goal

Having a sense of purpose can provide direction and motivation, especially during tough times. If that purpose is rooted in faith in God, it can help us push beyond our limitations and stay focused on our goals. To come out of our shells, we need to have a goal and a purpose.

Living a Life Of Impact

Empowering others is a key aspect of coming out of our shells. By mentoring, delegating, and encouraging those around us, we not only foster their growth but also expand our impact. Leadership is about building up others and creating a legacy of shared success. Moses empowered others, including Aaron, Joshua, and the elders of Israel, to take on leadership roles. He shared his responsibilities and mentored the next generation (Exodus 18; Numbers 27:18-20).

The story of Moses is a powerful reminder that breaking out of our shells is essential for realizing our potential and fulfilling our purpose. By embracing our identity, overcoming fear and doubt, accepting leadership roles, learning from challenges, trusting in a higher purpose, and empowering others, we can transform our lives and those around us.

Moses' journey from a hesitant shepherd to a great leader demonstrates that anyone can rise above their limitations and make a significant impact. Let his story inspire you to step out of your comfort zone, face your fears, and embrace the extraordinary path that awaits you.

Chapter 9
Get Back On Track

Life's journey is often filled with detours and setbacks. The stories of Joseph and Samson from the Bible provide powerful examples of how to get back on track after experiencing significant challenges. Joseph's rise from slavery and imprisonment to becoming a ruler in Egypt, and Samson's redemption after a fall from grace, offer valuable lessons on resilience, faith, and perseverance.

Joseph's life was marked by a series of misfortunes. Sold into slavery by his jealous brothers and later imprisoned on false charges, he faced overwhelming adversities. However, Joseph remained resilient, using his circumstances to develop his skills and maintain his faith in God's plan (Genesis 37; 39; 40 & 41).

Samson, blessed with immense strength, was destined to deliver Israel from the Philistines. However, his life took a downward spiral due to personal weaknesses and poor choices, culminating in his betrayal by Delilah and subsequent capture by the Philistines (Judges 13-16).

Getting back on track is crucial before it's too late. Take Samson, for example, who rediscovered his path when he was at death's door. He turned to prayer for the first time as he sought revenge on his enemies (Judges

16:28). This act of seeking divine guidance is often the best way to get back on track. Similarly, Joseph found his way by acknowledging his maker early in life. We must learn from their examples and take corrective actions before it's too late. In this discussion, we'll explore key factors that can help us get back on track and restore our momentum.

Resilience

Resilience is key to getting back on track after setbacks. Embracing resilience means staying committed to your goals, learning from your experiences, and continually striving to improve. Whether you are facing career challenges, rejections, personal issues, or health problems, resilience allows you to navigate through adversity and emerge stronger.

Faith

Despite the injustice he faced, Joseph maintained his faith in God. He believed that God had a purpose for his suffering and trusted in His timing. This faith was ultimately rewarded when he was appointed as Pharaoh's second-in-command, enabling him to save his family and many others from famine (Genesis 41-45).

After losing his strength and sight, Samson got his faith rekindled. Imprisoned and humiliated, he prayed to God for one final act of strength to defeat the

Philistines. His faith was answered, and he brought down the temple, killing many of Israel's enemies and delivering a decisive blow to the Philistines (Judges 16:28-30).

Maintaining faith and hope during difficult times can provide the strength and motivation needed to get back on track. Believing in a higher purpose or having confidence in your abilities can guide you through tough situations. Faith can be a source of inner strength, offering comfort and direction when you need it most.

Re-Awaken Your Talents

Joseph's ability to interpret dreams and his administrative skills played a crucial role in his rise to power. Even in prison, he utilized his talents to help others, which eventually led to his introduction to Pharaoh (Genesis 40-41). Samson's physical strength was his defining talent. Although he misused his gift at times, his final act of strength was a testament to his potential when aligned with a greater purpose (Judges 16:30). Everyone has unique skills and talents that can be leveraged to overcome obstacles and achieve success. Identify your strengths and find ways to apply them, even in challenging circumstances. Utilizing your talents can open new doors and create opportunities for personal and professional growth.

Learn To Navigate

While Joseph didn't make significant mistakes in his story, he did learn to navigate complex social and political environments. His early experiences taught him humility and patience, which were crucial in his later success (Genesis 37, 39, 40 & 41).

Samson's story is filled with mistakes, particularly his trust in Delilah and his arrogance regarding his strength. However, his final act was one of redemption, demonstrating that it is never too late to learn from past errors and make amends (Judges 16:28-30). Mistakes are an inevitable part of life. What matters is how you respond to them. Reflect on your experiences, understand where you went wrong, and make the necessary adjustments. Learning from mistakes is crucial for personal development and getting back on track.

Joseph found favor with those in positions of authority, such as Potiphar and the prison warden, which helped him navigate his difficult circumstances. He also reconciled with his family, which was instrumental in the preservation of his lineage (Genesis 39-45). In his final moments, Samson called upon God for strength, showing his dependence on divine support. This act of humility and reliance on a higher power was key to his redemption (Judges 16:28).

Seek Support

Seeking and accepting support from others can provide the necessary resources and encouragement to overcome setbacks. Whether it's leaning on faith, friends, family, or mentors, support systems are vital for getting back on track.

The stories of Joseph and Samson taught us that setbacks and failures are not the end of the journey. By embracing resilience, maintaining faith, utilizing our talents, learning to navigate, and seeking support, we can get back on track and fulfill our potential. These biblical narratives inspire us to rise above our challenges and continue striving toward our goals, no matter how difficult the path may seem.

Chapter 10
Move On

Apostle Paul, one of the most influential figures in the New Testament, embodied the essence of moving on from the past and embracing a new life of purpose and mission. His dramatic conversion from a persecutor of Christians to a devoted apostle of Christ offers profound lessons on how to leave behind our old ways and move forward with conviction and determination.

Paul, originally known as Saul, was a fervent persecutor of Christians. His encounter with Jesus on the road to Damascus was a pivotal moment that transformed his life (Acts 9:1-19). This experience marked the beginning of his journey as a dedicated follower of Christ.

Embrace Transformation

Embrace the possibility of transformation. No matter how entrenched you are in your current situation or past mistakes, a significant change is always possible. Paul's dramatic conversion teaches us that it's never too late to turn our lives around and pursue a new direction.

Reflection

Reflection is very crucial in getting back on track. Samson had a reflection of his past. Reflection gives us a glimpse of the past and helps us identify our mistakes. We need to reflect on areas of our lives where we feel stuck or regretful. Identify the changes you need to make and take decisive steps toward transformation. To reiterate this, 2 Cor 13:5 states:

> *Examine yourselves to see whether you are in the faith; test yourselves. Do you not realize that Christ Jesus is in you—unless, of course, you fail the test?*

Whether it's a career change, a shift in personal habits, or a new approach to relationships, it's important to examine ourselves in the process of becoming a better version. Paul had a tumultuous past that included persecuting Christians. After his conversion, he chose not to dwell on his previous actions but instead focused on his new mission. He wrote, "Forgetting what is behind and straining toward what is ahead, I press on toward the goal" (Philippians 3:13-14).

Let Go of the Past Hurts

Letting go of past hurts is essential for moving forward. Holding onto past mistakes or grievances can hinder your progress and prevent you from embracing new opportunities. We need to embrace self-forgiveness and release any lingering guilt or resentment. Focus on the present and the future, rather than being weighed down by past failures or regrets. This mindset will free you to pursue new goals with energy and optimism. Once Paul embraced his new identity, he pursued his calling with unparalleled passion. He traveled extensively, preaching the gospel and establishing churches despite facing significant opposition and hardships (Acts 13-28).

Find your calling

Find your calling and pursue it with passion. Paul's dedication to his mission, despite the obstacles, demonstrates the power of a clear and compelling purpose. Identify what you are passionate about and what gives your life meaning. Commit to pursuing this purpose wholeheartedly, even when faced with challenges. Passion and perseverance are key to achieving lasting fulfillment and making a meaningful impact. Paul's journey was fraught with adversity, including imprisonment, shipwrecks, and physical assaults. Despite these challenges, he adapted to each situation and continued his mission with unwavering faith (2 Corinthians 11:23-28).

Be Flexible

Adaptability and resilience are crucial for overcoming adversity. Paul's ability to remain steadfast in his mission, regardless of the circumstances, teaches us to remain flexible and resilient in the face of change. Develop a mindset of adaptability. When confronted with unexpected changes or setbacks, look for ways to adjust your plans and continue moving forward. Resilience and the ability to adapt will help you navigate through life's inevitable ups and downs.

Form Strong Partnerships

Paul worked closely with other believers, forming strong partnerships with figures like Barnabas, Silas, and Timothy. These relationships provided mutual support and encouragement (Acts 11-16). A supportive community is vital for personal growth and mission fulfillment. Paul's collaborations highlight the importance of surrounding yourself with like-minded individuals who can offer support and encouragement. Build a network of supportive relationships. Seek out mentors, friends, and colleagues who share your values and goals. A strong support system can provide valuable guidance, encouragement, and assistance as you pursue your path.

Paul's ultimate goal was to spread the gospel and glorify God. He remained focused on this mission throughout his life, even in the face of death. His letters often reflect this singular focus, encouraging others to live with an eternal perspective (2 Timothy 4:7-8).

Maintain a Clear Focus

Maintaining a clear focus on your ultimate goal helps you stay on track, even during challenging times. Paul's life teaches us the importance of keeping our eyes on the prize and not getting distracted by temporary setbacks. Define your long-term goals and keep them in mind as you navigate through daily challenges. Let your ultimate purpose guide your decisions and actions, providing a steady direction and motivation.

Apostle Paul's journey from a persecutor to a passionate apostle of Christ exemplifies the power of transformation, resilience, and purpose. By embracing these lessons, we can learn to let go of the past, pursue our calling with passion, adapt to change, and stay focused on our ultimate goals. Paul's life encourages us to move on from our past limitations and embrace a future filled with possibility and purpose.

Chapter 11
Stand Up and Save Others

Biblical stories abound with powerful examples of people rising above personal challenges to make a significant impact on the lives of others. Stories like those of Joseph, Samson, the Apostle Paul, and even Moses highlight the importance of courage, leadership, and selflessness in serving others. This chapter uses these stories to highlight the importance of standing up to save others.

Embrace Your Calling

Even after he was unfairly convicted and sold into slavery, Joseph embraced his special talent of dream interpretation. In addition to helping him become influential, his gift allowed him to prevent a major famine from striking Egypt and his family (Genesis 41–45). Moses, on the other hand, finally accepted his position as the leader of the Israelites despite his initial reluctance. His people were freed from Egyptian slavery as a result of his acceptance of his mission (Exodus 3–4). Finding and following your calling may have a significant impact on others around you as well as on yourself. Being aware of your place in the larger scheme of things can enable you to contribute in a meaningful way, whether via special abilities or a feeling of purpose.

Identify your passions and areas of strength, then think about how you can utilize them to benefit others. Embrace opportunities to be a leader and a supporter, knowing that your actions can have a domino effect that improves many lives.

Overcome Personal Challenges

Paul experienced many hardships such as incarceration and persecution, but his unshakable faith and commitment to sharing the gospel played a crucial role in the founding of the first Christian communities (Acts 13–28). Samson's ultimate act of redemption demonstrated how conquering one's obstacles may result in great triumphs for others despite his shortcomings and the loss of his strength (Judges 16:28-30). Reaching your personal goals is essential to putting yourself in a position to assist others.

Those who want to arise must possess resilience and the ability to persevere in the face of difficulty. Recognize and deal with your issues to grow and get better. Make use of your past experiences to help and empathize with those who are going through similar things. Your journey through difficulties might serve as a valuable source of motivation and support.

Act With Courage And Determination

It took tremendous courage and determination for Moses to face Pharaoh and guide the Israelites across the Red Sea (Exodus 14). Paul showed unmatched bravery and dedication to his cause by continuing on his missionary travels even after being aware of the risks (2 Corinthians 11:23-28). It takes courage and tenacity to defend the rights of others.

To stand up against injustice, take chances, and make tough choices that are in the best interest of society as a whole requires courage. By venturing outside of your comfort zone and acting boldly when necessary, you will develop bravery and defend people who are unable to defend themselves by speaking out against injustice. Your tenacity has the power to motivate people to support your cause and bring about long-lasting change.

Lead By Example

Joseph showed the value of leading by example when he brought Egypt out of famine and made reconciliation with his family by upholding his moral principles and applying wisdom (Genesis 41–45). While Paul's life and teachings shaped the early Christian church and many others by serving as a compelling example of faith, tenacity, and devotion (Philippians 3:13–14).

You establish an example for people to follow by your deeds, honesty, and dedication. Lead with honesty and model the behavior you want to see. Demonstrate the ideals and values you uphold by your conduct. Being an example for others allows you to inspire and encourage others to do good deeds.

Build And Empower a Supportive Community

Paul's partnerships with Barnabas, Silas, and Timothy highlight the value of creating community support to accomplish shared objectives (Acts 11–16). Moses demonstrated the value of shared leadership by giving leaders like Joshua and the elders the authority to help guide the Israelites (Numbers 27:18–20). For long-lasting effects, a community must be established and empowered. A network of support multiplies efforts and creates a sense of unity and purpose within the group. Concentrate on establishing solid, dependable connections within your neighborhood. Give people opportunities to participate and acknowledge their abilities to give them a sense of empowerment. A strong, cohesive society can do more as a unit than as one individual.

Focus On The Greater Good

The deeds of Joseph, motivated by his desire to save his family and the Egyptian people, highlight the need to keep the bigger picture in mind (Genesis 45:5-8). Paul's objective was to strengthen communities and preach the gospel, exhibiting a life devoted to a greater good (2

Timothy 4:7-8). Keeping the greater good in mind gives one drive and direction. A person's aspirations should be in line with the overarching objective of helping others and having a good influence. Make sure your objectives are in line with other people's needs. Give priority to deeds that advance the common good and consider all relevant factors while making judgments. Your work has the potential to have a significant, long-term effect on the community and beyond.

The stories of Joseph, Samson, Paul, and Moses illustrated that standing up to save others requires embracing your calling, overcoming personal challenges, acting with courage, leading by example, building a supportive community, and focusing on the greater good. By internalizing these lessons, we can rise to the occasion and make a meaningful difference in the lives of others. Let these biblical narratives inspire you to step up, take action, and contribute to the well-being and growth of those around you.

Chapter 12
Confess, Proclaim And Declare It

Psalm 62:11 declares:

One thing God has spoken, two things I have heard: "Power belongs to you, God.

You will agree with me that there is power in the word. The Bible says "For the word of God is living and active, sharper than any two-edged sword, piercing to the division of soul and spirit, of joints and marrow, and discerning the thoughts and intentions of the heart" (Heb 4;12). That means in His word is life. Hence, the word of God is a veritable tool to overcome unpalatable circumstances. It is a weapon that can command into existence that which is not in existence. It has the potency of creation. The scripture reiterates in Isaiah 45:11 that we should command him concerning the works of His hands.

Recently, I was faced with a situation that seemed like all hope was gone. I cried unto God to bring normalcy to that particular situation, and he heard my cry, and He did exactly what I wanted in the order of Sarah (Gen: 22:11). Are you facing a situation that makes you afraid? Prophet Isaiah confessed in Isaiah 59:19 that when the enemy shall come in like a flood, the Spirit of the LORD shall lift a standard against him. Furthermore, David in Psalm 46:5 declares that God is in the midst of her; she shall not be moved; God shall help her, and that right early.

The above scriptures are sure arsenals to confess when going through challenges. Having this confidence is to the effect that whenever we are overwhelmed with life issues, we have a redeemer who lives and who is attentive to hear our cry.

I could remember the testimony of a man of God so many years ago about someone who was about to give up the ghost. During that time, the man of God stated a bible verse came to his mind, which happened to be Psalm 79:11 that says:

> *Let the sighing of the prisoner come before thee, according to the greatness of thy power, deliver those that are appointed to die.*

He said as soon as he declared that scripture, the dead person was jacked back to life. The word is potent.

Are you feeling downcast within you? Declare God's word in Hebrew 13:5b "the Lord will never leave or forsake me. After all, He has said in His word that he would help us right early (Psalm 46:5). This is a sweet assurance.

I was once discussing with my cousin, and she mentioned that she usually looks for a word in the scripture to make her request. She gave me Psalm 68:6b(KJV) as a weapon she usually declares when praying. It says:

God setteth the solitary in families: he bringeth out those which are bound with chains:

One of the Psalms I love is Psalm 91 vs. 1-3. It reads:

He that dwelleth in the secret place of the Most High Shall abide under the shadow of the Almighty. I will say of the LORD, He is my refuge and my fortress: My God; in him will I trust. Surely he shall deliver thee from the snare of the fowler, And from the noisome pestilence.

These are words of reassurance in times of trouble. We can access the throne of mercy and obtain mercy in times of need (Heb 4:16). Hence, we only need to be timely to obtain the sure mercies of David when due. After all, the bible has declared, we shall decree a thing, and it shall be established: and light shall shine upon our ways (Job 22:28). God is desirous of our proclamation. He only acts on what we declare, confess, and proclaim.

Do not get tired of proclaiming His word over that situation. Do not let past hurts and challenges drive you out of the way of God. Make sure you proclaim it and be expectant of that which the word of God would do in your life.

Is your marriage deviating from the will of God? I Sam 2:9a has declared that he will keep the feet of his saints. In addition, he has also declared peace in the storm (Mark 4:39). Therefore, you need not exercise fear. If you believe, His peace will locate your home once again.

Are you finding it difficult to get a job? He has said in his words that the favor of the Lord, God, shall be upon us, and He shall establish the work of our hands (Psalm 90:17). I see you getting congratulated soon as you are about to be handed a gainful employment.

Are you finding it hard to excel in your academics? He has promised you success, but you must do your part by studying at the right time. The secret of my academic success over the years has been my total reliance on God, a strong will, and my determination to study to show myself approved.

Do not hesitate to proclaim and declare peace in that situation. I once shared in this book how I had one issue that almost took away my peace. There is a solution in the word of God for every problem. I kept on declaring the word until it accomplished that what it was sent to do. In God's word, there is absolute peace. The Psalmist said, *I will listen to what God will say, for he will speak peace to his people, let them not return to folly* (Psalm 85:8). I am delighted to inform you that after reminding God of all His promises in the word of God, He brought peace into that situation.

You can speak and confess His words, and He will bring to pass all the beautiful things He has said about you. Once you speak the word into existence, be assured things will begin to turn around and there will be an overturning in your favour (Ezek 21:27). I see you moving out from self pity, past hurts and retrogression and advancing into the fulfilment of God's promises.

Till I come your way again, keep soaring and keep enlarging.

*

If you benefited from this book, please consider posting an online review. Thank you in advance.

About the Author

Rufus Adeoluwa Olodude is a multifaceted individual with a passion for law, education, and career counselling. He is a lawyer, scholar, researcher, arbitrator, educator, and author. He has been a convener of Christian seminars, an editor of Christian magazines, and a teacher of God's word.

His first book, titled *Purposeful Generation* was a call on youths to live meaningful and purposeful lives. In the book, he admonishes the youth to have a renewed mindset for a take-over generation.

With academic excellence and professional distinctions, Rufus holds a Second Class Upper Division degree in Bachelor of Laws from the University of Ilorin and a Master of Laws with distinction from Obafemi Awolowo University, Ile-Ife. He also possesses a postgraduate diploma in education amongst other qualifications, and is also an Associate Member of the Chartered Institute of Arbitrators, United Kingdom.

Rufus' commitment to making a positive impact shines through his service in the Christian community and his dedication to helping others deepen their relationship with God. His teachings and writings have been a source of inspiration for many.

Follow the author on social media

Facebook: https://www.facebook.com/olodude.ade-oluwa?mibextid=ZbWKwL

Instagram: http://instagram.com/olodudeadeoluwa/

About the Publisher

Sulis International Press publishes select fiction and nonfiction in a variety of genres under four imprints:

- Riversong Books (fiction)
- Sulis Press (general nonfiction)
- Keledei Publications (spirituality)
- Sulis Academic Press (academic works)

For more, visit the website at
https://sulisinternational.com

Subscribe to the newsletter at
https://sulisinternational.com/subscribe/

Follow on social media
https://www.facebook.com/SulisInternational
https://twitter.com/Sulis_Intl
https://www.pinterest.com/Sulis_Intl/
https://www.instagram.com/sulis_international/

www.ingramcontent.com/pod-product-compliance
Lightning Source LLC
Chambersburg PA
CBHW032129090426
42743CB00007B/529